EDMONDS

CAKES

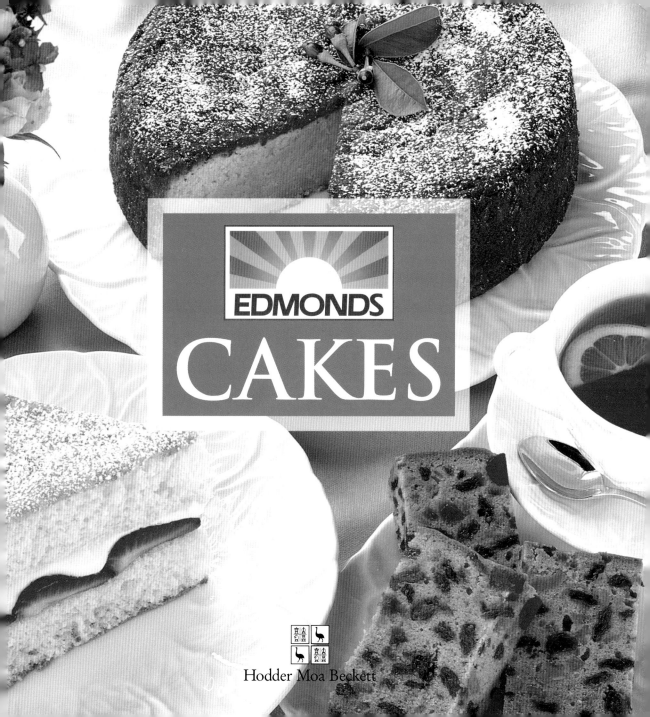

EDMONDS
CAKES

Hodder Moa Beckett

CONTENTS

INTRODUCTION

Welcome to the first title in the new range of Edmonds "mini" titles. Since 1907, Edmonds has helped many New Zealand cooks produce wonderful, tasty treats for family and friends alike. This tradition continues with these new books which explore individual styles of baking and cooking.

Included throughout *Cakes* are traditional Edmonds recipes that can also be found in the standard *Edmonds Cookery Book*, but we have also introduced a number of contemporary recipes that allow the cook to produce tempting treats for every occasion.

Mouthwatering photography accompanies the recipes – and we certainly hope these tempt you to try all the recipes in the book.

We would love to hear your comments on this new title in the Edmonds range, so feel free to write to Bluebird Foods Limited, Private Bag, Manukau City, Auckland.

From all the Edmonds Team, we wish you many hours of great baking!

ALMOND CRUMBLE CAKE

125 g butter, softened

¾ cup caster sugar

2 eggs

¼ teaspoon almond essence

1½ cups Champion standard grade flour

2 teaspoons Edmonds baking powder

70 g pkt ground almonds

1 cup milk

CRUMBLE TOPPING

½ cup Champion standard grade flour

2 tablespoons brown sugar

70 g pkt sliced almonds

¼ cup melted butter

Cream butter and sugar until light and fluffy. Add eggs one at a time, beating well after each addition. Beat in almond essence. Sift together flour and baking powder. Fold into creamed mixture alternately with ground almonds and milk. Spoon into a greased 20 cm round cake tin that has the base lined with baking paper. Scatter crumble topping over cake. To make the topping, combine all ingredients in a bowl. Mix well. Bake at 180°C for 50–55 minutes or until a skewer inserted in the centre of the cake comes out clean. Leave cake in tin for 15 minutes before turning onto a wire rack.

Almond Crumble (top centre)
Banana Cake (right)
Butter Cake (left)

BANANA CAKE

125 g butter, softened

¾ cup sugar

2 eggs

1½ cups mashed ripe bananas (about 4 medium bananas)

1 teaspoon Edmonds baking soda

2 tablespoons hot milk

2 cups Champion standard grade flour

1 teaspoon Edmonds baking powder

Lemon Icing (page 58)

lemon zest to garnish

Cream butter and sugar until light and fluffy. Add eggs one at a time, beating well after each addition. Add mashed banana and mix thoroughly. Stir soda into hot milk and add to creamed mixture. Sift flour and baking powder. Fold into mixture. Turn into a greased and lined 20 cm round cake tin. Bake at 180°C for 50 minutes or until cake springs back when lightly touched. Leave in tin for 10 minutes before turning out onto a wire rack. When cold, ice with Lemon Icing and garnish with lemon zest.

VARIATION

The mixture can be baked in two 20 cm round sandwich tins at 180°C for 25 minutes. The two cakes can be filled with whipped cream and sliced banana.

BUTTER CAKE

150 g butter, softened
1 teaspoon vanilla essence
¾ cup sugar
2 eggs
1½ cups Champion standard grade flour
3 teaspoons Edmonds baking powder
¾ cup milk, approximately
icing sugar to dust

Cream butter, vanilla and sugar until light and fluffy. Add eggs one at a time, beating well after each addition. Sift flour and baking powder together. Fold into creamed mixture. Add sufficient milk to give a soft dropping consistency. Spoon mixture into a greased and lined deep 20 cm round cake tin. Bake at 180°C for 35–40 minutes or until cake springs back when lightly touched. Leave in tin for 10 minutes before turning out onto a wire rack. When cold, dust with icing sugar.

CAPPUCCINO CAKE

150 g butter

¾ cup sugar

3 egg yolks

1½ cups Champion standard grade flour

2 teaspoons Edmonds baking powder

½ cup strong black coffee, cooled

1 teaspoon cinnamon

TOPPING

3 egg whites

¾ cup caster sugar

Melt butter in a saucepan large enough to mix all the ingredients. Remove from heat and stir in sugar and egg yolks. Fold in sifted flour and baking powder alternately with coffee. Place mixture in a 20 cm round springform tin lined on the base with baking paper. Spread topping over. To make the topping, beat egg whites until stiff. Gradually beat in sugar and continue beating until mixture is thick. Bake at 180°C for 45–50 minutes or until an inserted skewer comes out clean. Cool in tin before releasing the sides of the tin. Cool. Dust with cinnamon.

CARROT CAKE

3 eggs

1 cup sugar

¾ cup vegetable oil

2 cups Champion standard grade flour

1 teaspoon Edmonds baking powder

1 teaspoon Edmonds baking soda

½ teaspoon cinnamon

3 cups grated carrots

¾ cup (225 g can) drained unsweetened crushed pineapple

½ cup chopped walnuts

1 teaspoon grated orange rind (optional)

Cream Cheese Icing (page 58)

orange zest to garnish

Beat together eggs and sugar for 5 minutes until thick. Add oil and beat for 1 minute. Sift flour, baking powder, baking soda and cinnamon. Combine carrot, pineapple, walnuts and orange rind. Fold into egg mixture. Fold in dry ingredients. Grease a deep 20 cm ring tin. Line base with baking paper. Spoon mixture into tin. Bake at 180°C for 50–55 minutes or until a skewer inserted in the centre of the cake comes out clean. Leave in tin for 10 minutes before turning out onto a wire rack. When cold, spread with Cream Cheese Icing and garnish with orange zest.

EDMONDS

CHOCOLATE CAKE

(WITH BLACK FOREST VARIATION PHOTOGRAPHED)

175 g butter, softened
1 teaspoon vanilla essence
1¾ cups sugar
3 eggs
2 cups Champion standard grade flour

½ cup cocoa
2 teaspoons Edmonds baking powder
1 cup milk
Chocolate Icing (page 58) or icing sugar

Cream butter, vanilla essence and sugar until light and fluffy. Add eggs one at a time, beating well after each addition. Sift together cocoa, flour and baking powder. Fold into creamed mixture alternately with milk. Spoon mixture into a greased and lined 22 cm round cake tin. Bake at 180°C for 55–60 minutes or until a skewer inserted in the centre comes out clean. Leave in tin for 10 minutes before turning out onto a wire rack. When cold, ice with Chocolate Icing or dust with icing sugar.

BLACK FOREST CAKE

Chocolate Cake (recipe above)
Chocolate Ganache:
100 g dark chocolate, chopped
2 tablespoons cream

¼ cup Kirsch
250ml cream, whipped
425 g can stoneless black cherries, thoroughly drained

To make the ganache, place chocolate and cream in a small saucepan. Stir over a low heat until chocolate has melted and the mixture is smooth. Cool. Cut cake horizontally into 3 layers. Place one layer on a serving plate. Brush liberally with Kirsch. Spread with half the cream then arrange half the cherries on top. Repeat with another layer of cake, Kirsch, cream and cherries. Top with final layer of cake. Spread ganache over top of cake.

CHOCOLATE CHERRY BRANDY CAKE

425 g can stoneless black
cherries, drained and halved
¼ cup brandy
2 tablespoons brown sugar
100 g dark cooking chocolate,
coarsely chopped
175 g butter, softened
1 cup sugar
2 cups Champion
high grade flour

3 eggs
2 tablespoons cocoa
2 teaspoons Edmonds baking
powder
¼ cup milk

CHOCOLATE ICING
100 g dark cooking chocolate,
chopped
50 g butter

Combine cherries, brandy, brown sugar and chocolate. Set aside to marinate while preparing the cake. Cream the butter and sugar until light and fluffy. Add eggs one at a time, beating well after each addition. Sift flour, baking powder and cocoa together. Fold into creamed mixture alternately with milk. Gently fold in cherries and chocolate mixture. Spoon mixture into a greased and lightly floured 23 cm gugelhupf (ribbed ring tin) or a deep 23 cm ring tin. Bake at 180°C for 45 minutes or until cake springs back when lightly touched. Leave cake in tin for 10 minutes before turning out onto a wire rack. When cool, dribble hot chocolate icing over the cake using a spoon. To make the icing, melt the chocolate and butter together over a pot of hot water, stirring constantly until smooth.

CHOCOLATE CHIP SPECKLE CAKE

175 g butter, softened
1½ cups sugar
4 eggs
1 teaspoon vanilla essence
1½ cups Champion standard grade flour
1½ teaspoons Edmonds baking powder
¾ cup chocolate chips

Cream butter and sugar until light and fluffy. Add eggs one at a time, beating well after each addition. Beat in vanilla. Sift together flour and baking powder. Fold into creamed mixture with chocolate chips. Spoon mixture into a well-greased 22 cm baba tin. Bake at 180°C for 55–60 minutes or until a skewer inserted in the centre of the cake comes out clean. Leave cake in tin for 10 minutes before turning onto a wire rack.

CHRISTMAS CAKE

1¾ cups orange juice

¾ cup dark rum or brandy

2 tablespoons grated orange rind

500 g currants

500 g raisins

400 g sultanas

2 cups chopped dates

150 g crystallised ginger, chopped

150 g packet mixed peel

150 g glace cherries, halved

½ teaspoon vanilla essence

¼ teaspoon almond essence

2 teaspoons grated lemon rind

1 cup blanched almonds

2½ cups Champion high grade flour

½ teaspoon Edmonds baking soda

1 teaspoon cinnamon

1 teaspoon mixed spice

½ teaspoon ground nutmeg

250 g butter, softened

1½ cups brown sugar

2 tablespoons treacle

5 eggs

In a saucepan, bring to the boil orange juice, rum and orange rind. Remove from heat and add dried fruit. Cover and leave fruit to soak overnight. Stir vanilla and almond essences, lemon rind and almonds into saucepan. Sift flour, soda and spices into a bowl. In a separate large bowl, cream butter, sugar and treacle until light and fluffy. Add eggs one at a time, beating well after each addition. Into this mixture fold sifted ingredients alternately with fruit mixture. Line a deep, square 23 cm tin with two layers of brown paper followed by one layer of baking paper. Spoon mixture into tin. Bake at 150°C for 4 hours or until an inserted skewer comes out clean when tested. Cover the tin with a piece of brown paper for the first 2 hours of the cooking time to prevent the top of the cake browning too quickly. Leave in tin until cold. Wrap in foil. Store in a cool place. Ice if wished.

CINNAMON PECAN CAKE

100 g pecan nuts
125 g butter, softened
1 cup caster sugar
2 eggs
1 teaspoon vanilla essence
1½ cups Champion standard grade flour
1½ teaspoons Edmonds baking powder
1 teaspoon cinnamon
¾ cup milk

COFFEE CREAM FILLING
75 g butter, softened
1 cup icing sugar
1 teaspoon instant coffee
icing sugar to dust

Place pecan nuts in a food processor. Pulse until ground. Cream butter and sugar until light and fluffy. Add eggs one at a time, beating well after each addition. Beat in vanilla. Fold in ground pecans. Sift together flour, baking powder and cinnamon. Fold into creamed mixture alternately with milk. Spoon into a greased 20 cm round cake tin that has had the base lined with baking paper. Bake at 180°C for 45 minutes, or until a skewer inserted in the centre of the cake comes out clean. Leave cake in tin for 10 minutes before turning onto a wire rack. When cold, split cake in half horizontally. Place one half on a serving plate. Spread over Coffee Cream Filling then sandwich with remaining half of cake. To make the filling, beat together butter, icing sugar and coffee until smooth. Dust cake with icing sugar. If desired, cut star shapes out of baking paper and place on top of the cake before dusting with icing sugar.

Cinnamon Pecan Cake (below right)
Citrus Sour Cream Cake (below left)
Coconut Cake (top)

CITRUS SOUR CREAM CAKE

125g butter, softened

1 teaspoon grated lemon rind

1 teaspoon grated orange rind

1 cup sugar

3 eggs

1 cup Champion standard grade flour

1 teaspoon Edmonds baking powder

½ cup sour cream

tiny citrus leaves and orange rind to garnish

Cream butter, lemon rind, orange rind and sugar together until light and fluffy. Add eggs one at a time and beat well. Sift flour and baking powder together. Fold sifted ingredients into egg mixture alternately with sour cream, mixing until smooth. Pour mixture into a greased 20 cm round cake tin lined on the base with baking paper. Bake at 160°C for 45 minutes or until cake springs back when lightly touched. Leave in tin for 10 minutes before turning out onto a wire rack. Garnish with tiny citrus leaves and orange rind.

COCONUT CAKE

250 g butter, softened
1½ cups caster sugar
4 eggs
1 teaspoon vanilla essence
2 cups Champion standard grade flour
2 teaspoons Edmonds baking powder
1 cup desiccated coconut
White Icing (page 58)
toasted thread coconut to garnish

Cream butter and sugar until light and fluffy. Add eggs one at a time, beating well after each addition. Beat in vanilla essence. Sift together flour and baking powder. Fold flour and coconut into creamed mixture. Spoon into a greased deep 24 cm ring tin that has had the base lined with baking paper. Bake at 180°C for 45 minutes or until a skewer inserted in the cake comes out clean. Leave cake in tin for 10 minutes before turning onto a wire rack. When cold, spread with White Icing and garnish with toasted coconut.

COFFEE CAKE

250 g butter, softened

1½ cups caster sugar

3 eggs

2 cups Champion standard grade flour

2 teaspoons Edmonds baking powder

2 tablespoons coffee and chicory essence

¾ cup milk

Coffee Icing (page 58)

Cream butter and sugar until light and fluffy. Add eggs one at a time, beating well after each addition. Sift together flour and baking powder. Combine essence and milk. Fold dry ingredients and milk alternately into creamed mixture. Spoon into a deep 22 cm round cake tin that has had the base lined with baking paper. Bake at 180°C for 50–55 minutes or until a skewer inserted in the centre of the cake comes out clean. Leave cake in tin for 10 minutes before turning onto a wire rack. When cold, spread with Coffee Icing.

CONTINENTAL APPLE CAKE

250 g butter, melted

1¼ cups sugar

3¼ cups Champion standard grade flour

6 teaspoons Edmonds baking powder

4 eggs

2 large Granny Smith apples, peeled, cored and sliced

½ cup sultanas

2 tablespoons sugar

2 teaspoons cinnamon

1 teaspoon almond essence

icing sugar to dust

whipped cream or yoghurt to serve

Put butter, first measure of sugar, flour, baking powder and eggs into a bowl. Beat with an electric mixer on high speed until smooth. In a separate bowl combine apple slices, sultanas, second measure of sugar, cinnamon and almond essence. Spoon two-thirds of the batter into a greased and lined 25 cm round cake tin. Arrange the apple mixture on top. Spoon remaining batter over apple mixture. Bake at 180°C for 40–45 minutes or until cake is risen and golden. Leave in tin for 10 minutes before turning out onto a wire rack. Dust with icing sugar. Serve with cream or yoghurt.

DATE LOAF

1 cup chopped dates

1 cup boiling water

1 teaspoon Edmonds baking soda

1 tablespoon butter

1 cup brown sugar

1 egg, beaten

1 cup chopped walnuts

¼ teaspoon vanilla essence

2 cups Champion standard grade flour

1 teaspoon Edmonds baking powder

Put dates, water, soda and butter into a bowl. Stir until butter has melted. Set aside for 1 hour. Beat sugar, egg, walnuts and vanilla into date mixture. Sift flour and baking powder into date mixture, stirring just to combine. Pour mixture into a greased 22 cm loaf tin. Bake at 180°C for 45 minutes or until loaf springs back when lightly touched. Leave in tin for 10 minutes before turning onto a wire rack.

FIELDER'S SPONGE

3 no. 7 eggs, separated
½ cup caster sugar
½ cup Edmonds Fielder's cornflour
2 teaspoons Champion standard grade flour
1 teaspoon Edmonds baking powder

Beat egg whites until stiff. Gradually add the sugar, beating continuously until mixture is stiff and sugar has dissolved. Add egg yolks and beat well. Sift cornflour, flour and baking powder. Carefully fold into egg mixture with a metal spoon. Pour into two 20 cm sandwich tins lined on the base with baking paper. Bake at 190°C for 15–20 minutes or until cake springs back when lightly touched. Leave in tin for 5 minutes before turning out onto a wire rack.

Serving suggestion: Sandwich sponges together with whipped cream and hulled, halved strawberries. Dust with icing sugar.

Fielder's Sponge (below left)
Fruit Cake (below right)
Lemon Curd and Yoghurt Cake (top)

FRUIT CAKE

675 g mixed fruit

¼ cup mixed peel

3 tablespoons Champion high grade flour

225 g butter

1 cup brown sugar

2 tablespoons golden syrup

1 tablespoon marmalade

5 eggs, beaten

3 cups Champion high grade flour

1 teaspoon Edmonds baking powder

pinch of salt

1 teaspoon mixed spice

½ teaspoon ground nutmeg

Combine mixed fruit and peel in a bowl. Dust with the first measure of flour. Cream butter, sugar and golden syrup until light and fluffy. Stir in marmalade. Sift the second measure of flour, baking powder, salt, mixed spice and nutmeg together. Add flour and eggs alternately to creamed mixture. Add prepared fruit and mix well. Line a deep, 20 cm square cake tin with two layers of brown paper followed by one layer of baking paper. Spoon mixture into cake tin, smoothing the surface. Bake at 150°C for 2–2½ hours or until an inserted skewer comes out clean. Leave in tin until cold.

LEMON CURD AND YOGHURT CAKE

250 g butter, softened

1½ cups caster sugar

4 eggs

finely grated zest of 1 lemon

2 cups Champion standard grade flour

2 teaspoons Edmonds baking powder

½ cup lemon curd (see recipe below)

¾ cup natural unsweetened yoghurt

icing sugar to dust

citrus leaves to garnish

whipped cream to serve

Cream butter and sugar until light and fluffy. Add eggs one at a time, beating well after each addition. Beat in lemon zest. Sift flour and baking powder together. Combine lemon curd and yoghurt. Fold dry ingredients into creamed mixture alternately with lemon curd mixture. Spoon into a deep 22 cm round cake tin that has been greased and lined with baking paper. Bake at 180°C for 50–55 minutes. Cool in tin. Dust with icing sugar and garnish with citrus leaves. Serve with cream.

LEMON CURD

50 g butter

¾ cup sugar

1 cup lemon juice

2 eggs, beaten

1 teaspoon finely grated lemon zest

Melt the butter in the top of a double boiler. Stir in sugar and lemon juice until sugar is dissolved. Add eggs and lemon zest. Place over boiling water and cook, stirring all the time until mixture thickens. Cool. Store in the refrigerator in a covered container.

LEMON SEMOLINA CAKE

3 tablespoons Champion standard grade flour

¾ cup Fleming's semolina

4 eggs

½ cup sugar

1 tablespoon grated lemon rind

SYRUP

1 cup sugar

½ cup water

¼ cup lemon juice

1 teaspoon grated lemon rind

In a bowl combine flour and semolina. Separate the eggs. Beat egg yolks and sugar together until pale and thick. Gently fold semolina mixture and lemon rind into egg mixture. Beat egg whites until peaks just fold over. Fold a quarter of egg whites into egg mixture, then remaining egg whites. Pour mixture into a 20 cm round springform tin lined on the base with baking paper. Bake at 180°C for 40 minutes or until a skewer inserted in centre of cake comes out clean. Leave in tin for 10 minutes before transferring to a serving plate. To make the syrup, place sugar, water, lemon juice and rind in a small saucepan. Heat gently, stirring constantly until sugar has dissolved. Pour hot syrup over cake about a quarter at a time, leaving time for the cake to soak up the syrup.

MACAROON CAKE

100 g butter
½ cup sugar
3 egg yolks
1½ cups Champion standard
grade flour
2 teaspoons Edmonds baking
powder
½ cup milk

1 teaspoon vanilla essence
½ cup raspberry jam

TOPPING
3 egg whites
¾ cup caster sugar
1½ cups coconut
1 teaspoon almond essence

Melt butter in a saucepan large enough to mix all the ingredients. Stir in sugar and egg yolks. Sift flour and baking powder into the saucepan. Add milk and vanilla essence and mix with a wooden spoon to combine. Spoon mixture into a 20 cm round springform tin lined on the base with baking paper. Spread jam over batter. Spread topping over jam. To make the topping, beat egg whites until stiff. Gradually beat in sugar and continue beating until mixture is thick. Mix in coconut and almond essence. Bake at 180°C for 45–50 minutes or until an inserted skewer comes out clean. Cool in tin for 10 minutes before releasing the sides of the tin.

MADEIRA CAKE

250 g butter, softened
1 cup sugar
½ teaspoon grated lemon rind
4 eggs
2¼ cups Champion standard grade flour
1½ teaspoons Edmonds baking powder

Cream butter and sugar until light and fluffy. Stir in lemon rind. In a separate bowl beat eggs until thick. Sift flour and baking powder together. Add to creamed mixture alternately with the eggs. Stir to mix. Spoon mixture into a 20 cm square cake tin lined on the base with baking paper. Bake at 180°C for 30 minutes or until the cake springs back when lightly touched. Leave in tin for 10 minutes before turning out onto a wire rack.

Madeira Cake (top right)
Marble Cake (bottom centre)
Moist Apple Walnut Cake (top left)

MARBLE CAKE

125g butter, softened

1 cup sugar

2 eggs

1½ cups Champion standard grade flour

1½ teaspoons Edmonds baking powder

¼ cup milk

2 tablespoons cocoa

2 drops red food colouring

Chocolate Icing (page 58)

Cream butter and sugar until light and fluffy. Add eggs one at a time, beating well after each addition. Sift together flour and baking powder. Fold into creamed mixture alternately with milk. Divide mixture into three equal parts. Into one portion stir the cocoa, and to another the food colouring. Leave the last portion plain. Spoon stripes of the three mixtures into a greased and lined 20 cm round cake tin. Bake at 180°C for 50 minutes or until a skewer inserted in the centre of the cake comes out clean. Leave in tin for 10 minutes before turning out onto a wire rack. When cold, spread with Chocolate Icing.

MOIST APPLE WALNUT CAKE

4 eggs

2 cups sugar

1 cup vegetable oil

1 cup roughly chopped walnuts

2 cups grated unpeeled Granny Smith apple (2 medium apples)

440 g can unsweetened crushed pineapple, drained

2 cups Champion standard grade flour

1½ teaspoons Edmonds baking powder

¾ teaspoon Edmonds baking soda

2 teaspoons cinnamon

1 teaspoon mixed spice

Cream Cheese Icing (page 58)

lemon zest to garnish

Using a wooden spoon beat together eggs, sugar and oil until sugar dissolves. Stir in walnuts, apple and pineapple. Combine flour, baking powder, soda and spices. Stir into egg mixture. Transfer to a greased deep 20 cm square cake tin that has had the base lined with baking paper. Bake at 180°C for 1¼ hours. Leave cake in tin for 15 minutes before transferring to a wire rack. When cold, spread with Cream Cheese Icing and garnish with lemon zest.

MUD CAKE

BASE
**200 g packet chocolate thin
biscuits**
75 g butter
½ cup chocolate hazelnut spread

CAKE
50 g butter
1 cup sugar
3 eggs

1 tablespoon vanilla essence
**1½ cups Champion standard
grade flour**
**3 teaspoons Edmonds baking
powder**
3 tablespoons cocoa
¼ cup boiling water
½ cup milk
icing sugar to dust
ready-made chocolate sauce

To make the base, crush biscuits into fine crumbs. Melt butter and mix into biscuit crumbs. Press over the base of a 20 cm round cake tin lined on the base with baking paper. Spread with hazelnut spread. To make the cake, melt butter in a saucepan large enough to mix all the ingredients. Remove from heat. Add sugar, eggs and vanilla. Sift flour and baking powder together. Mix cocoa into boiling water. Fold flour, cocoa mixture and milk into butter mixture. Pour over base. Bake at 180°C for 45–50 minutes, or until cake springs back when lightly touched. Cool in tin for 10 minutes before turning onto a wire rack. Dust with icing sugar and serve with chocolate sauce.

ORANGE POLENTA CAKE

125 g butter, softened

1 cup caster sugar

2 eggs

finely grated zest of 1 orange

¼ cup freshly squeezed orange juice

¼ cup orange marmalade

1 cup Champion standard grade flour

1 teaspoon Edmonds baking powder

½ cup polenta (cornmeal)

70 g pkt ground almonds

½ cup milk

orange zest to garnish

Cream butter and sugar until light and fluffy. Add eggs one at a time, beating well after each addition. Beat in orange rind, juice and marmalade. Sift flour and baking powder together. Fold flour, polenta, almonds and milk into creamed mixture. Spoon into a 20 cm round cake tin that has been greased and lined with baking paper. Bake at 180°C for 45 minutes or until a skewer inserted in the centre of the cake comes out clean. Leave cake in tin for 10 minutes before turning onto a wire rack. Garnish with orange zest.

EDMONDS

PANFORTE

1 cup hazelnuts, toasted, shelled and roughly chopped
1 cup blanched almonds, toasted and roughly chopped
½ cup dried figs, chopped
½ cup dried apricots, chopped
¼ cup crystallised ginger, chopped
¼ cup mixed peel
¾ cup Champion high grade flour
1 teaspoon cinnamon
¾ teaspoon ground nutmeg
¼ teaspoon ground cloves
½ cup runny honey
½ cup caster sugar

Thoroughly grease a 20 cm round cake tin. Line the base and sides with baking paper. Combine nuts, dried fruit, flour and spices in a mixing bowl. Mix well. Place honey and sugar in a small saucepan. Stir over a low heat until sugar dissolves. Bring to the boil, stirring constantly. Boil for about 2 minutes until mixture reaches the "soft ball" stage. To test for soft ball stage, drop a small amount of mixture off a teaspoon into cold water. When a soft ball forms, the mixture is ready. On a sugar thermometer, the soft ball stage is 116°C. Do not let the syrup change colour. Remove from the heat and let the bubbles subside. Carefully pour syrup over dry ingredients, then quickly mix to combine. Press into prepared tin. (Speed is vital, as the mixture will become sticky and unmanageable very quickly.) Bake at 150°C for 45 minutes in the lower third of the oven. Cool in tin. Wrap in foil and store in the refrigerator. To serve, cut into thin wedges.

RICH CHOCOLATE CAKE

(A very moist and rich flourless cake. Suitable for dessert.)

175 g unsalted butter, softened

¾ cup brown sugar

1 teaspoon vanilla essence

6 eggs, separated

150 g dark cooking chocolate, melted

2 x 70 g packets ground almonds

icing sugar

whipped cream

Cream butter, sugar and vanilla until light and fluffy. Beat in egg yolks. Fold in melted chocolate and almonds. In another bowl beat egg whites until soft peaks form. Gradually fold whites into chocolate mixture. Pour into a greased and lined 20 cm springform tin. Bake at 190°C for 20 minutes then reduce heat to 150°C for a further 35 minutes or until firm. Allow cake to cool in tin. Release cake and transfer to a serving plate. Dust with icing sugar and serve warm or cold with cream.

CHOCOLATE LIQUEUR CAKE

Omit vanilla essence and replace with 2 teaspoons chocolate, coffee or orange liqueur.

Rich Chocolate Cake (below left)
Tosca Cake (below right)
Sultana Cake (top)

SULTANA CAKE

2 cups sultanas
250 g butter, chopped in small pieces
2 cups sugar
3 eggs, beaten
½ teaspoon lemon essence or almond essence
3 cups Champion standard grade flour
1½ teaspoons Edmonds baking powder

Put sultanas in a saucepan. Cover with water. Bring to the boil then simmer for 15 minutes. Drain thoroughly. Add butter. In a bowl beat sugar into eggs until well combined. Add sultana mixture and essence. Sift flour and baking powder together. Mix sifted ingredients into fruit mixture. Spoon mixture into a greased and lined 20 cm square cake tin. Bake at 160°C for 1–1½ hours or until cake springs back when lightly touched. Leave in tin for 10 minutes before turning onto a wire rack.